KU-395-635

OUR LOCAL AREA

Living in a City

Richard Spilsbury

Heinemann
LIBRARY

www.heinemannlibrary.co.uk
Visit our website to find out more information about Heinemann Library books.

To order:

☎ Phone +44 (0) 1865 888066

🖹 Fax +44 (0) 1865 314091

🖥 Visit www.heinemannlibrary.co.uk

Edited by Charlotte Guillain and
  Catherine Veitch
Designed by Joanna Hinton-Malivoire
Original illustrations © Capstone Global Library
Illustrated by Joanna Hinton-Malivoire
Picture research by Elizabeth Alexander and
  Fiona Orbell
Originated by Dot Gradations Ltd
Printed in China by South China Printing Company Ltd

ISBN 978 0 431 02088 4 (hardback)
14 13 12 11 10
10 9 8 7 6 5 4 3 2 1

British Library Cataloguing in Publication Data
Spilsbury, Richard
Living in a city. – (Our local area)
910.9'1732-dc22
A full catalogue record for this book is available from the British Library.

Acknowledgements
We would like to thank the following for permission to reproduce photographs: Alamy pp. **10** (© Lyndon Giffard), **14** (© Alexander Caminada), **17** (© Adrian Sherratt), **19** (© Chad Ehlers); © Capstone Global Library Ltd. pp. **4**, **5**, **8**, **12** & **15** (Tudor Photography); Collections p. **11** (Richard Davis); Corbis pp. **9** (© Atlantide Phototravel/Corbis), **16** (© Hulton-Deutsch Collection), **18** (© Jon Hicks), **21** (© John Miller/Robert Harding World Imagery); Getty Images p. **7** (Jason Hawkes).

Cover photograph of traffic crossing a bridge over the River Aire in Leeds, Yorkshire, UK reproduced with permission of Alamy (© Leeds City Pictures/Paul Ridsdale).

We would like to thank Rachel Bowles for her invaluable help in the preparation of this book.

Every effort has been made to contact copyright holders of material reproduced in this book. Any omissions will be rectified in subsequent printings if notice is given to the publisher.

All the Internet addresses (URLs) given in this book were valid at the time of going to press. However, due to the dynamic nature of the Internet, some addresses may have changed, or sites may have changed or ceased to exist since publication. While the author and publisher regret any inconvenience this may cause readers, no responsibility for any such changes can be accepted by either the author or the publisher.

Contents

Any words appearing in the text in bold, **like this**, are explained in the glossary.

What is a city?

A city is a place where tens of thousands of people live. A city is much bigger than a town or village. Many places became cities because they had a **cathedral**, a very big and important church. Some of the 50 official British cities today have no cathedral, but each has a **charter** from the Queen. This recognizes each city as a large, important place.

This is a view across the rooftops of the city of Oxford. How many church towers can you spot?

Most cities were built long ago. People built many cities by rivers. In the past they used rivers to carry goods because there were not so many roads. People also used river water for drinking, cooking, and powering **watermills**.

City centres

Cities get bigger over time. Old buildings, such as the **cathedral** and city hall, are usually in the centre of the city. New buildings are built around the centre. Roads lead out from the centre to streets of newer buildings.

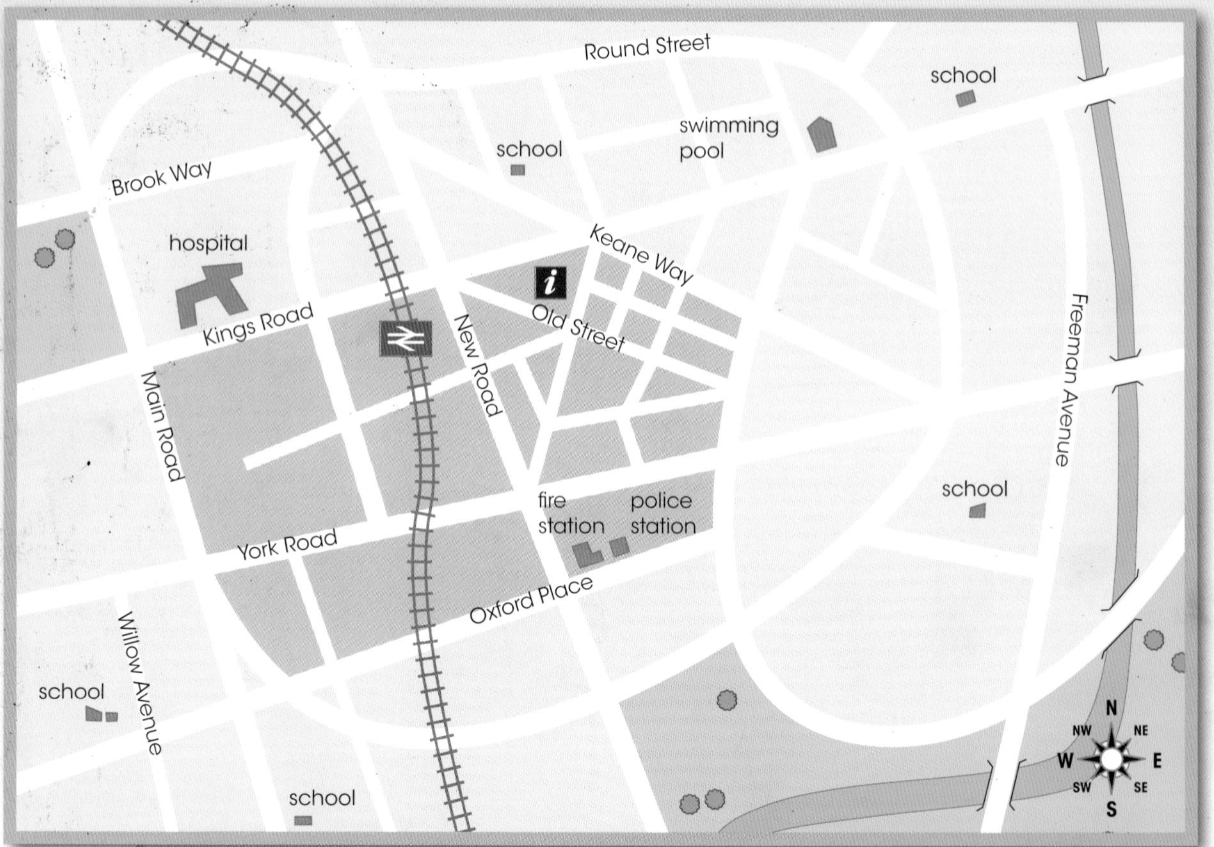

Round Street

school

swimming pool

school

Brook Way

hospital

Keane Way

Kings Road

Old Street

Main Road

New Road

Freeman Avenue

school

fire station

police station

York Road

Oxford Place

Willow Avenue

school

school

NW N NE
W   E
SW S SE

On this city plan the busy city centre is coloured grey. Can you point to the **ring road** people drive around to get past the centre?

The most important and usually the biggest city in a country is called the **capital** city. This amazing office tower is in London, the capital city of the United Kingdom.

Today, city centres are full of big shops, restaurants, and **offices**. Offices are often in tall, narrow buildings where many people work. Most people who live in cities live in houses and **flats** outside the centre. Their homes may be grouped in small areas, rather like villages, with small local shops.

City transport

Some commuters cycle to a station and catch a train into the city centre to work.

Many people travel into city centres every day to work. They are called **commuters**. Some commuters travel into the city by train, car, or bus. Some people ride bicycles across the city to work.

City roads are often crowded and busy. This means the traffic moves very slowly. London and some other cities have an underground railway line. The trains move smoothly between different places all across the city by going through long tunnels underground.

People can move across a city quickly on underground trains.

City days

In the daytime the city is full of people doing different jobs. Some people work in shops selling goods. Others work as receptionists, housekeepers, and chefs in hotels where city visitors stay. Police, firefighters, and ambulance workers keep the city safe. What jobs do people do in **offices** and banks?

Some workers, such as these window cleaners, keep the city clean.

There are many restaurants and cafes selling different types of food in a city. Some cities have a Chinatown. This is an area where there are many Chinese restaurants and shops.

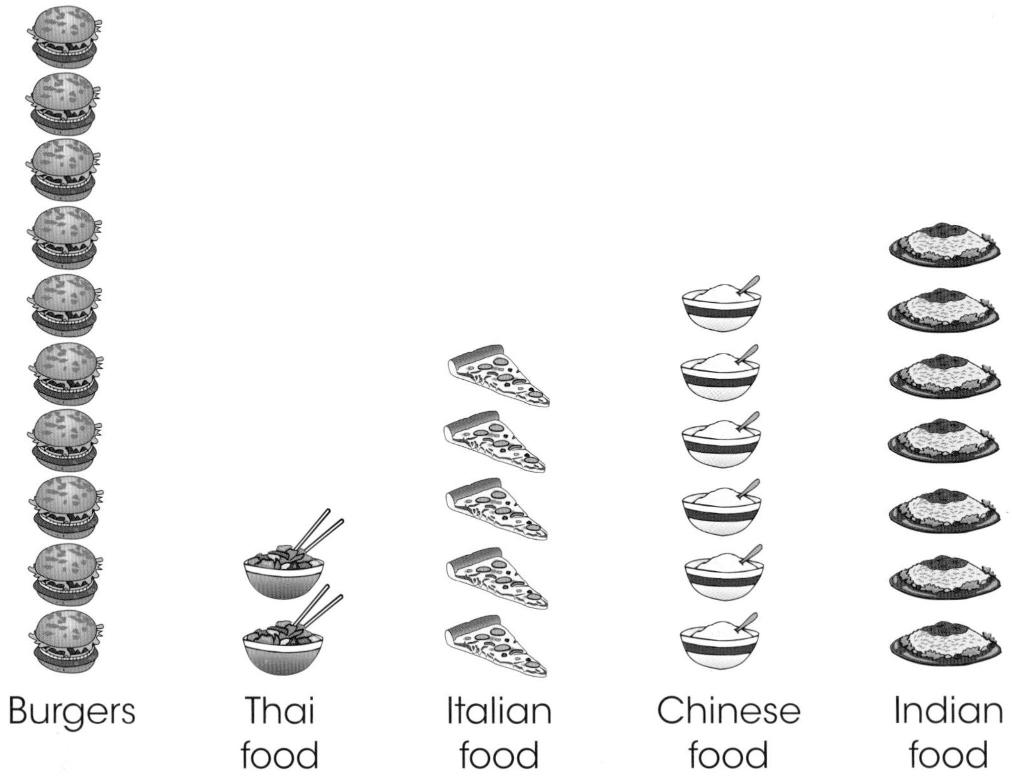

Burgers	Thai food	Italian food	Chinese food	Indian food

Sean and his class made a **pictogram**. It shows their favourite types of city restaurants. Which is the most popular? What is your favourite?

City fun

In a city there are lots of things to do. There are many cinemas and theatres where you can watch different films and shows. There are ice rinks, pools, and sport centres. A city has different **museums** that may have special displays, from dinosaurs to cars!

In this city museum, school children are having a close look at old bones.

Most cities have outdoor spaces where people can relax.

In the summer people have picnics in city parks, or they go boating on lakes. In **public gardens** there are lots of beautiful plants to see. In summer, some people leave the city and visit the countryside to find more space, peace, and quiet.

In the past

Canals used to be important transport routes in the city.

In the past, **canals** were built in some cities. People used boats on the canals to carry goods to and from the city. Along the canals there were **factories** making goods. The canals were busy, working places.

In city centres, people sometimes change what old buildings are used for. For example, when a bank or prison closes down, people sometimes make a restaurant or a hotel inside the building. What are the oldest buildings left in your local area and how have they been changed over the years?

Today, canals are busy with visitors. People take boat trips and visit shops and restaurants on old canal boats.

Global cities

The oldest parts of cities can look very different to each other. Varanasi in India is built on the River Ganges. This river is special to **Hindus**, and in Varanasi there are over 2,000 Hindu **temples**, mostly at the river's edge. The modern parts of cities, with **offices** and shops, often look similar.

Can you see any ways in which Varanasi is similar and different to where you live?

Tokyo in Japan is the biggest megacity in the world. Using an **atlas**, can you find the next four biggest megacities?

The biggest 25 cities in the world are called **megacities**. More than ten million people live and work in each megacity. That is about one-sixth of the total number of people who live in the whole of the United Kingdom.

Likes and dislikes

Jemma likes the shops, the parks, and all the things to do in her city. But she thinks the city is too busy and crowded. She says the cars on the roads make the air dirty.

Likes	Dislikes
shops	crowds
zoo	traffic
park	long journey to school
theatre	
cycling	litter on streets

When there is too much traffic it can take a long time to travel across a city. Traffic also causes air pollution.

Some people say that cities need more cycling lanes. Then more people would cycle instead of going by car. People could also share car rides so there are fewer cars on the roads. How would you change a city to make it nicer to live in?

On the Underground

Below is an underground train map. The different routes are shown in different colours. Which colour train lines would you take to get from High Hill to Church Street? (Clue: You have to change once.)

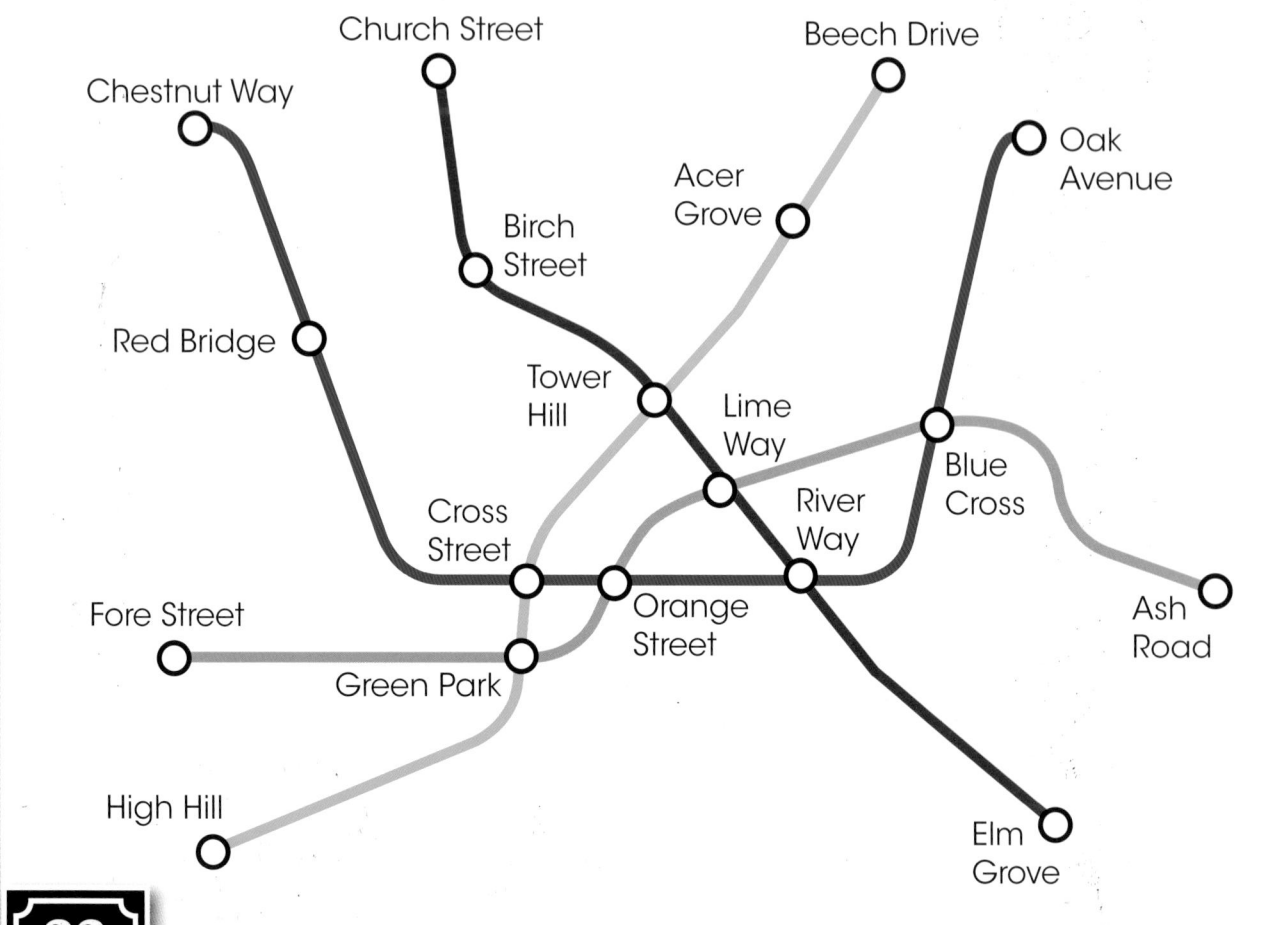

Glossary

atlas book containing maps and information about the world

canal straight, water-filled channels dug by people, often for boats to move along

capital most important, and usually the biggest, city in a country

cathedral large and important Christian church

charter document giving permission for something to be built

commuters people who travel regularly between home and work

department store large shop with different departments within it

factory building where people make or process things to sell

flat apartment, usually containing several rooms on one floor of a larger building

Hindu person who follows the religion of Hinduism. Hindus believe in lots of different gods.

megacity city where more than ten million people live

museum building in which people collect, study, and look after rare or interesting objects for other people to see

offices rooms where people work

pictogram graph showing symbols of objects, such as fruit or shops

public garden park which is open for all people to visit

ring road road built around a city centre

temple place where people worship

watermill building where grain is ground into flour using the power of water

Index

Find out more

Books to read

Living in Cities (Where People Live), Neil Morris (Smart Apple Media, 2004)

City Homes (Homes around the World), Nicola Barber (Crabtree, 2007)

Websites

BBC Schools, City tours
www.bbc.co.uk/schools/twocities/
Use this site to explore the differences between two cities, Belfast in the UK and Mexico City in Central America.